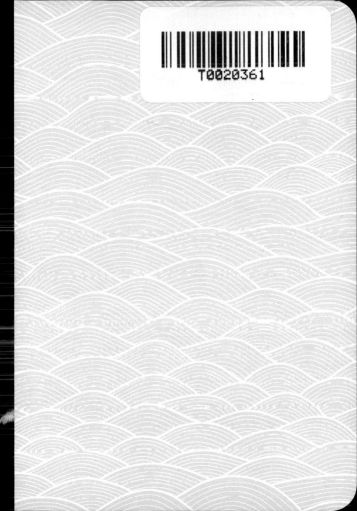

I LOVE YOU
DAD

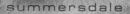
summersdale

I LOVE YOU DAD

Summersdale Publishers Ltd
46 West Street
Chichester
West Sussex
PO19 1RP
UK

www.summersdale.com

Printed and bound in China

ISBN: 978-1-84953-858-9

Substantial discounts on bulk quantities of Summersdale books are available to corporations, professional associations and other organisations. For details contact Nicky Douglas by telephone: +44 (0) 1243 756902, fax: +44 (0) 1243 786300 or email: nicky@summersdale.com.

TO...

FROM...

MY FATHER GAVE
ME THE GREATEST
GIFT ANYONE
COULD GIVE
ANOTHER PERSON:
HE BELIEVED IN ME.

Jim Valvano

MY FATHER'S BUSY BUT HE ALWAYS HAS TIME FOR ME.

Judy Blume

YOU HAVE TAUGHT
ME SO MUCH.

ANY MAN CAN
BE A FATHER,
BUT IT TAKES A
SPECIAL PERSON
TO BE A DAD.

Anonymous

LIFE DOESN'T
COME WITH AN
INSTRUCTION BOOK;
THAT'S WHY WE
HAVE FATHERS.

H. Jackson Brown Jr

I FEEL LIKE I CAN
DO ANYTHING WITH
YOU BY MY SIDE.

MIGHTY OAKS FROM LITTLE ACORNS GROW.

Proverb

DAD: A SON'S FIRST
HERO, A DAUGHTER'S
FIRST LOVE.

Anonymous

YOU MAKE ME
FEEL FEARLESS.

A FATHER IS
SOMEONE YOU
LOOK UP TO, NO
MATTER HOW
TALL YOU ARE.

Anonymous

ANYONE WHO
TELLS YOU
FATHERHOOD IS
THE GREATEST
THING THAT
CAN HAPPEN TO
YOU, THEY ARE
UNDERSTATING IT.

Mike Myers

I KNOW THAT
YOU WILL ALWAYS
SUPPORT ME.

HE DIDN'T TELL
ME HOW TO LIVE;
HE LIVED, AND
LET ME WATCH
HIM DO IT.

Clarence Budington Kelland

I LOVE MY
FATHER AS THE
STARS – HE'S A
BRIGHT SHINING
EXAMPLE AND A
HAPPY TWINKLING
IN MY HEART.

Adabella Radici

THANK YOU FOR
ALWAYS BELIEVING IN
ME, ESPECIALLY WHEN
I DOUBT MYSELF.

IF YOUR CHILDREN
LOOK UP TO YOU,
YOU'VE MADE A
SUCCESS OF LIFE'S
BIGGEST JOB.

Anonymous

I CANNOT THINK
OF ANY NEED
IN CHILDHOOD
AS STRONG AS
THE NEED FOR
A FATHER'S
PROTECTION.

Sigmund Freud

YOU INSPIRE ME TO
ALWAYS BE BRAVE.

ONE'S FAMILY
IS THE MOST
IMPORTANT
THING IN LIFE.

Robert Byrd

ONE FATHER
IS MORE THAN
A HUNDRED
SCHOOLMASTERS.

George Herbert

YOU ARE ALWAYS
THERE FOR ME, NO
MATTER WHAT.

CHILDREN LEARN
TO SMILE FROM
THEIR PARENTS.

Shinichi Suzuki

NO MAN I EVER
MET WAS MY
FATHER'S EQUAL,
AND I NEVER
LOVED ANY
OTHER MAN
AS MUCH.

Hedy Lamarr

YOU TELL
THE WORST
(BUT BEST)
JOKES.

TO HER, THE
NAME OF FATHER
WAS ANOTHER
NAME FOR LOVE.

Fanny Fern

THERE IS MORE TO
FATHERS THAN MEETS
THE EYE.

Margaret Atwood

WE HAVE BEEN
ON SOME OF THE
BEST ADVENTURES.

THERE'S NO
PILLOW QUITE
SO SOFT AS A
FATHER'S STRONG
SHOULDER.

Richard L. Evans

THE FAMILY IS
ONE OF NATURE'S
MASTERPIECES.

George Santayana

YOU TAUGHT ME
HOW TO LOVE
AND BE LOVED
IN RETURN.

FATHERING IS
NOT SOMETHING
PERFECT MEN DO,
BUT SOMETHING
THAT PERFECTS
THE MAN.

Frank Pittman

WHEN MY FATHER
DIDN'T HAVE
MY HAND... HE
HAD MY BACK.

Linda Poindexter

YOU GIVE THE
GREATEST HUGS.

MY DAD IS MY
HERO. I'M NEVER
FREE OF A
PROBLEM NOR DO I
TRULY EXPERIENCE
A JOY UNTIL
WE SHARE IT.

Nancy Sinatra

A MAN'S CHILDREN
AND HIS GARDEN
BOTH REFLECT THE
AMOUNT OF WEEDING
DONE DURING THE
GROWING SEASON.

Anonymous

YOU ARE ALWAYS
PATIENT AND
UNDERSTANDING.

FAMILY IS NOT AN
IMPORTANT THING.
IT'S EVERYTHING.

Michael J. Fox

A FATHER IS A
GIANT FROM WHOSE
SHOULDERS YOU
CAN SEE FOREVER.

Perry Garfinkel

YOU ALWAYS
KNOW WHAT
TO SAY IN ANY
SITUATION.

THE MARK OF A
GOOD PARENT IS
THAT HE CAN
HAVE FUN WHILE
BEING ONE.

Marcelene Cox

FAMILIES ARE LIKE FUDGE — MOSTLY SWEET, WITH A FEW NUTS.

Anonymous

YOU ALWAYS HAVE
MY BEST INTERESTS
AT HEART.

IT IS A WISE
FATHER THAT
KNOWS HIS
OWN CHILD.

William Shakespeare

A FATHER'S
WORDS ARE LIKE
A THERMOSTAT
THAT SETS THE
TEMPERATURE
IN THE HOUSE.

Paul Lewis

I CAN TRUST YOU
WITH ANYTHING.

NO MAN STANDS
SO TALL AS WHEN
HE STOOPS TO
HELP A CHILD.

Abraham Lincoln

YOU WILL ALWAYS
BE YOUR CHILD'S
FAVOURITE TOY.

Vicki Lansky

YOU CAN FIX
ABSOLUTELY
ANYTHING.

THE SECRET OF FATHERHOOD IS TO KNOW WHEN TO STOP TICKLING.

Anonymous

NO LOVE IS
GREATER THAN
THAT OF A FATHER
FOR HIS SON.

Dan Brown

YOU CONSTANTLY
ENCOURAGE ME TO BE
A BETTER PERSON.

A DAD IS SOMEONE
WHO WANTS TO
CATCH YOU BEFORE
YOU FALL, BUT
INSTEAD PICKS
YOU UP, BRUSHES
YOU OFF AND LETS
YOU TRY AGAIN.

Anonymous

ARE WE NOT LIKE
TWO VOLUMES
OF ONE BOOK?

Marceline Desbordes-Valmore

YOU ARE ALWAYS
PROUD OF MY
ACHIEVEMENTS.

MY FATHER WAS
MY TEACHER.
BUT MOST
IMPORTANTLY HE
WAS A GREAT DAD.

Beau Bridges

NOTHING YOU DO FOR CHILDREN IS EVER WASTED.

Garrison Keillor

THANK YOU
FOR TEACHING
ME EVERYTHING
YOU KNOW.

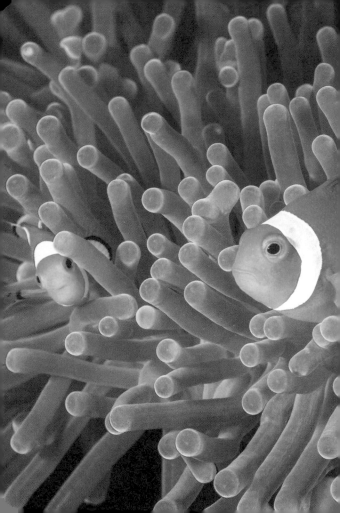

WHAT DO I OWE MY
FATHER? EVERYTHING.

Henry van Dyke

YOU ALWAYS
LISTEN.

WHILE WE TRY
TO TEACH OUR
CHILDREN ALL
ABOUT LIFE, OUR
CHILDREN TEACH
US WHAT LIFE
IS ALL ABOUT.

Angela Schwindt

MY FATHER USED
TO SAY THAT
IT'S NEVER TOO
LATE TO DO
ANYTHING YOU
WANTED TO DO.

Michael Jordan

I LOVE YOU
DAD.

If you're interested in finding out more about our books, find us on Facebook at **Summersdale Publishers** and follow us on Twitter at **@Summersdale.**

www.summersdale.com

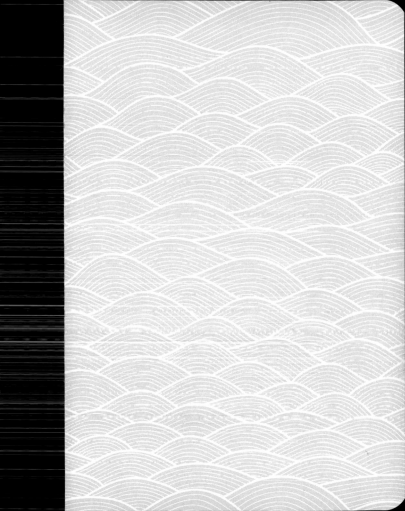